You Are Your Happiness

SHARAM

EDITED BY

Shahed & Nafiseh

TALIA

YOU ARE YOUR HAPPINESS

SHARAM

Edited by: Shahed & Nafiseh
Paperback 1st Edition
Published in 2017 by:

TALIA

Talia, Friends of Existence, Inc.
Website: www.taliafriends.org
Email: talia@taliafriends.org

Many thanks to Melina H & Stefan Hoelscher for their invaluable help.
Cover Art & Paintings: Sharam

More Books
by Sharam

Mysticism
The Psychology of Love

Happiness
The Essence of Your Being

Decoding Love
Understanding is Compassion

The Book of Existence
Part One

From Negativity to Joy

The Power of Let-Go

Don't Beat Yourself Up

available on
SharamLove.com

Mystical T-Shirts, Mugs &
Paintings by Sharam at
SharamLove.com

Follow us on Instagram:
@sharamlove

THE GLOSSARY

While reading,
if you come across
a mystical concept
you are unfamiliar with,
there is a glossary
at the end of the book
for reference.

INTRODUCTION

There is nothing as exciting as getting to know yourself. Every time we get an understanding of who we are, of why we do the things we do or react to things the way we do, we get a taste of freedom. We get a taste of life without limitation and we feel so much joy. From the moment we are born, our parents, unknowingly limit us with dos and don'ts. Don'ts create guilt in us, while dos puff up our ego, because we are doing the right thing. Between our ego and guilt, we become very limited. We lose our spontaneity. We enter each moment with prior rules and ideas, so we cannot be free. This goes on for our entire life.

Growing up or maturing means to become aware of these limitations by watching how they impact us in our lives. By becoming aware of our limitations, they can no longer trick us into living by their rules or restrictions. Our souls are as big as the universe, but like the moon eclipsing the sun, the soul is eclipsed by this tiny dead thing called ego. Awareness shines light on this dead thing so we can see it for what it is, a creator of misery and darkness.

Each page of *You Are Your Happiness* contains simple words of wisdom brought together to aid you on your journey to happiness and joy. You can read it front to back or pick a page each day on which to focus. At the end of the book, you will find a simple technique you can do to develop more awareness and joy in your life.

If you want to ask for help
with your growth from above,
you can, but you don't really
need to because someone has
already been assigned to help
you, and that person is you!

2

We can overcome any issue by
becoming aware of it. Becoming
aware of something means to bring
it out of the unconscious. We have no
power over issues that we have buried
in the unconscious. They seem bigger
than we are. When we become aware,
the power is in our hands. Awareness
makes everything clear to us. We can
see, and we gain power over
whatever we see.

When we accept, our energy doesn't get wasted in falling apart and throwing temper tantrums. We have more energy to focus on seeing ourselves and our egos. Acceptance is a must to have more energy. If we have more energy, that energy goes toward deeper understanding of the self, to awareness, and to turning ignorance into inner knowledge. It helps us to *not* put our identity on the ego. So when we accept, we have more energy to really work on ourselves.

You cannot go into your
wounds with anger, hatred,
or sadness and gain
understanding of them.
To heal your wounds you
have to enter them with
interest, happiness
and patience.

Happiness is a gift from God
that only *we* can give to ourselves.

One never becomes happy;
it is more that unhappiness
disappears, and we realize
that happiness was there all
the time. Happiness is natural.
Unhappiness is made by the
ambitious mind.

If you postpone happiness,
you will postpone it forever.

8

Humans might all look like one species on the outside, but inside, they are as different as an elephant is from an anteater. We accept differences in animal species; we don't mind them, but we don't accept humans the way they are. We want them all to be alike and act in certain ways. Maybe this understanding will help us accept humans as they are. After all, nobody asks anteaters why they eat ants.

Having expectation
means not giving space
to others. We give space
to strangers more than
we do to people who are
close to us.

Misery is the byproduct
of unconsciousness.

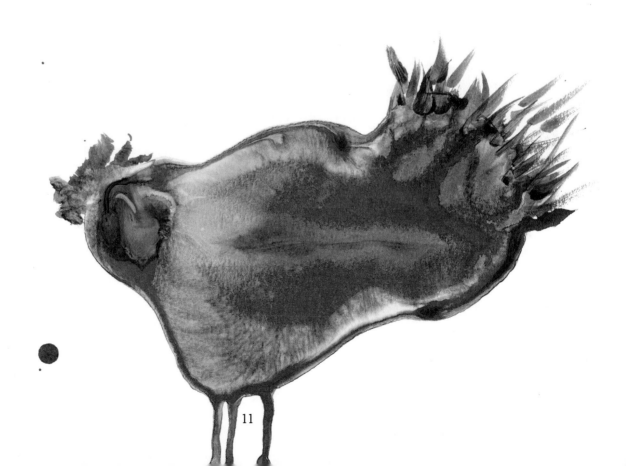

If we can make misery,
we can also understand
misery. Misery has
become our habit. If we
become alert, we can
get out of it.

12

When we defend ourselves,
we defend our habits.
We reinforce them and they
feel welcomed in our lives.
Furthermore, defending
itself has become a habit,
creating a vicious circle.

13

When we defend, we lose so much energy that we cannot understand anymore. We cannot grow because understanding that leads to growth requires a lot of energy.

14

One of the reasons we blame others is because we are under too much pressure. Pressure takes energy away from us. Without that energy, we don't have patience to look deeper into *our* issues. Instead, we get angry and blame others.

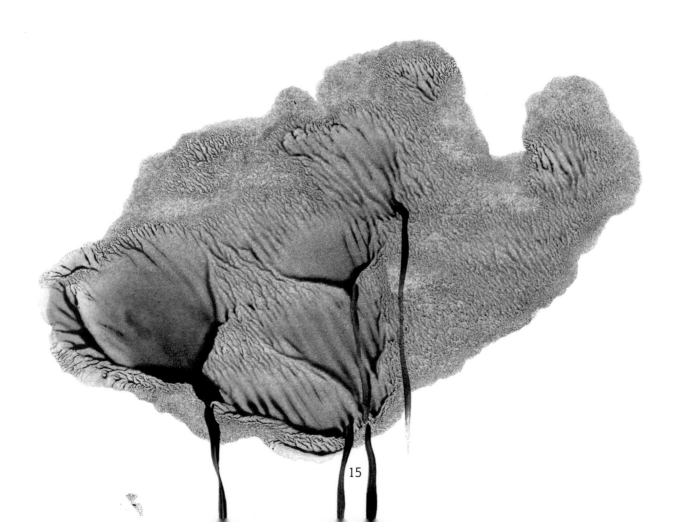

When we are positive, we don't get as much attention from others as when we are negative. That is why we are so invested in negativity. When we are positive, others want to get attention from us; but when our ego is gross and big, we don't want to give anything to anyone. Ego only wants to get something, not give. So wanting more attention means that in this moment I have a big ego—I am not mature; I am selfish and only want to get, not give.

Wanting attention is all about wanting to enjoy. As children, we get attention all the time. That attention moves our kundalini energy. As adults, we still want that juice, that energy, but because we are not kids anymore, we have to use our egos to get attention from others. Then we become dependent on others' attention to get just a little bit of energy. When we become aware, when we come to the moment, we have all our doors open and the energy floods in from everywhere.

When our kundalini energy moves, we don't have desires.
When kundalini energy arises, we become satisfied.
That is why desiring drops. Desire means not being satisfied
and looking for satisfaction outside ourselves.

A content person
is never disappointed.

Maturity means you stay in the moment. When you stay in the moment, you don't create wounds. So the more mature we are, the fewer wounds we have. The more immature we are, the more wounds.

20

If we do not have patience,
we throw a temper tantrum.
The definition of a temper
tantrum is simply being
impatient.

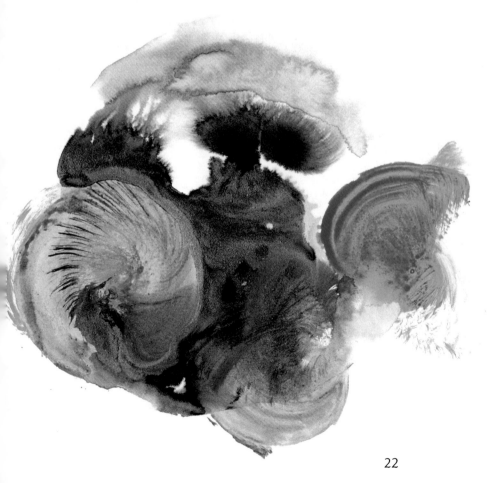

The only reason we get tired of being with people for a long time is because we feel we have to pay attention to them the whole time. Our mind has two parts. The part that wants to be with others, and the part that needs to be alone. These parts each have a certain capacity. Like sleeping and being awake—we need both. After a while, the part that wants to be with people becomes tired and we want to separate for a while and rest. But if we learn to be with others and not pay attention to them all the time, to disengage and be with ourselves for a while, then we don't have to separate from people. We can be with them for a long time and not get tired.

22

Why do we want to connect?
Because when we connect,
we put our ego aside.
We experience egolessness.

The only time you can connect
with someone is when you trust;
otherwise, there is no connection
between people. Trust means not
worrying, trusting that everything
that happens in Existence is
perfect. When you are not
worried, you open yourself;
you are relaxed and can connect.

If you are too afraid of conflict,
you will never love and
you will miss so much joy.

If we worry,
we become important
in the eyes of the ego.
If we are relaxed,
we are not important.

26

We worry so people will like us. Why? Society respects responsible people. If we worry about something, it shows that we care and feel responsible. If we are too carefree, if we laugh too much or are not serious enough, society sees us as irresponsible and looks down on us. But remember, worry doesn't help anything. It only harms us and those around us.

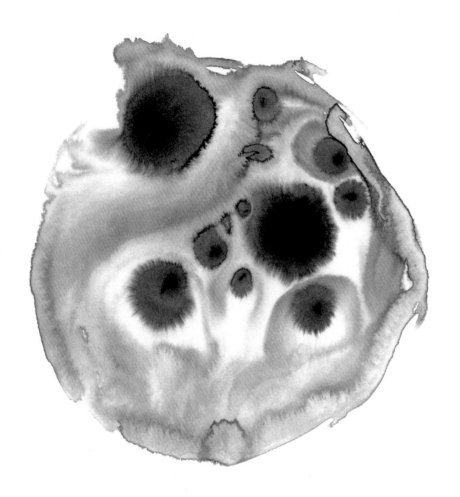

We want to be productive
so people will like us.

**Understanding gives us freedom
from the bondage of society.**

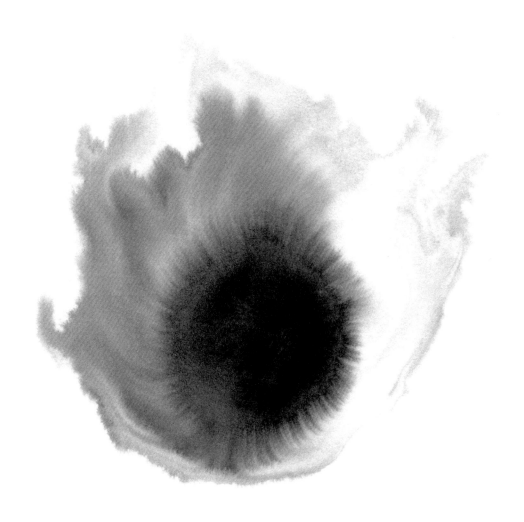

How do we let go of worry?
By remembering that
Existence does everything,
including whatever it is
you are worried about.

If you worry about tomorrow,
you ruin today *and* tomorrow.

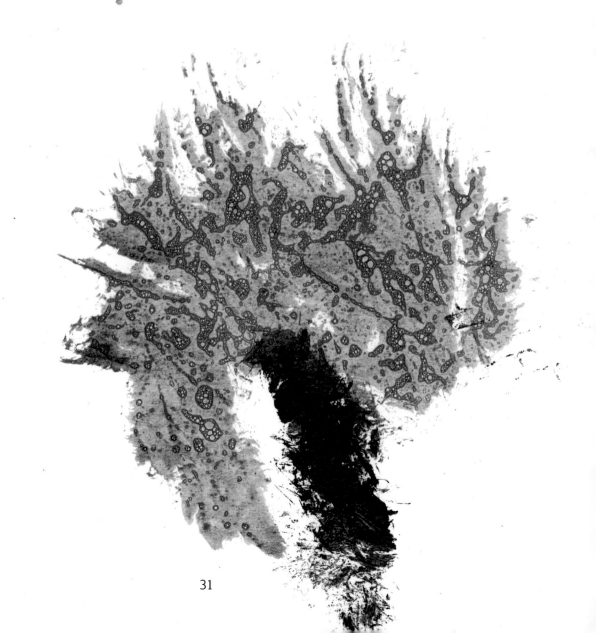

If our mind is in order,
everything around us
is in order.

No fact ever
hurts us,
it is only our
interpretations
of the facts
that create pain.

Unawareness makes
matters subjective,
dependent on
our point of view,
and we drown in them.
Awareness means
seeing things objectively.

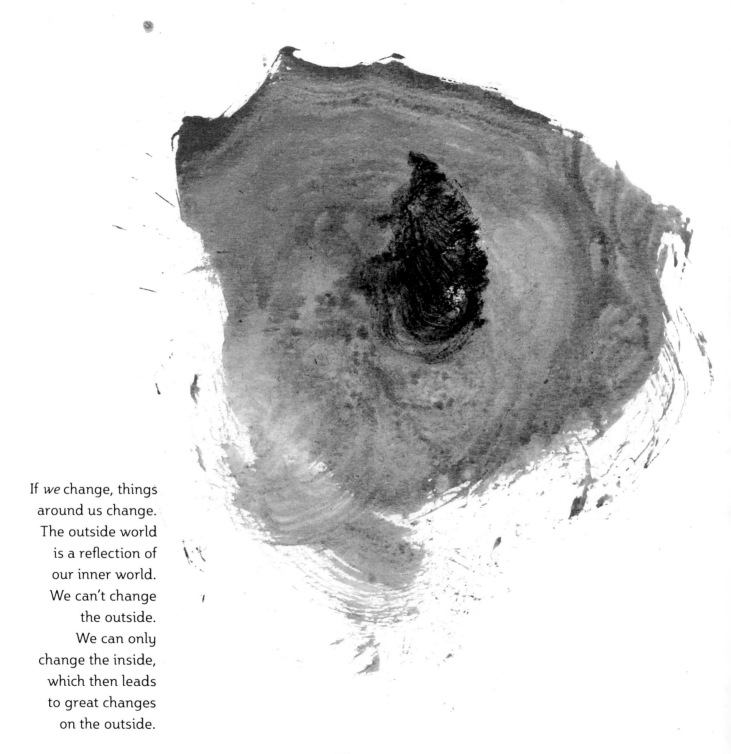

If *we* change, things
around us change.
The outside world
is a reflection of
our inner world.
We can't change
the outside.
We can only
change the inside,
which then leads
to great changes
on the outside.

**Your life exactly reflects
the way you think.**

At some level, people believe that they are victims of the life they have led and are currently living. They believe many of the things that have happened in their lives, things that have shaped who they are and their current circumstances, were out of their control. They don't understand that they created this life, detail by detail according to their subconscious, and that by becoming aware of their subconscious mind, they can change their circumstances at any time.

Sometimes the things
we want the most
are not the best for us,
while the things
we dislike the most, are.

38

In relaxation, the ego dies.
Why? Because the ego cannot
get any nourishment in relaxation.

The ego comes from believing in good and bad. With good comes greed—we want more of the good stuff—and with bad comes fear, so we want to avoid it.

40

Innocence happens when your
belief in good and bad leaves you.

We all have certain games that our egos play over and over again. For example, feeling not good enough, becoming emotional or bullying others to get our way, complaining all the time, being a good person so people will like us or being a bad person to rebel against our parents or society, and many, many others.

It is important to get to know our own games, so that we do not keep falling into them. If we do not get to know them, then we continue to see them as real, and we remain miserable. If we know our games and can begin to catch our ego playing them, then we can see them for what they are, just a game, and we won't fall into them.

42

When we fall into our emotional body and say, "I can't do it," what we really mean is, "I don't want to do it."

We think we are not worth anything; that is why we cling to others: friends, spouses, children.... We are afraid that no one else will want us. And, if those we cling to find out this is how we think, which they eventually will, they *will* want to escape. Only by knowing yourself, will you know your worth.

44

Knowing others
is wisdom.
Knowing yourself
is enlightenment.

Ego means being afraid of losing,
but we are only our soul;
everything else we have is borrowed.
So, if we don't have anything,
how can we lose it?

We fall to the first chakra
when we don't trust Existence.
Then we worry about money,
not having enough, and many
other things.

47

If, in one area of our life, we get something for free, or we steal something, we often will pay for it somewhere else because we feel guilty. That guilt brings us down and creates problems for us. For example, we steal something or take advantage of someone and all of a sudden we get a trafflc ticket with a big fine. There is always this balance in Existence. If we understand this and trust it, we won't steal or take advantage, because we know we will end up paying more for it later. It just is not worth it. The opposite is also true. When we feel absolutely trustworthy, we don't want to steal because we already feel so good; and because we feel so good about ourselves, Existence rewards us.

Also, as long as there is this feeling of stealing in us, we will stay poor, either inside or out. For example, if I don't have any money, I will remain penniless. If I have a million dollars in the bank and I steal, my wealth will not grow. I will stay at the same level, and even if I have that million dollars, I will still *feel* poor. All of this because we want to get something for free. So the choice is all yours—poverty and feeling poor or let go and abundance.

I do not want to say stealing is bad. I do not want to say anything is bad; it is the understanding that is important here. The understanding that if we have the feeling of wanting to steal, we do not allow ourselves to grow financially. We really feel poor. It does not matter how much we have. We want to take things to become happy, but the truth is that you become happy when you give. The best way to become happy and rich is to freely give.

Humans in general are ready to find something wrong with themselves, something to feel bad about or to make them feel inferior. All humans seek ways to prove that they are not good enough. This is another game of the ego.

When people do not like
themselves, they either become
very passive or very aggressive.
If you are more female and you
do not like yourself, you become
more passive, you withdraw.
If you are more male and you
do not like yourself, you
become aggressive.

If we get mad at someone,
we are still children inside
because we have given our
power to that person and we
think they have abused it.

We are afraid of making
mistakes because somebody
might put us down, but it is
only our ego that falls apart
if it gets judged.

We spend so much energy hiding our ego. We are afraid that if anybody sees it, they will attack it, and because we think we *are* our egos, we think *we* have been attacked. If we can let go of this hiding and fear, we will immediately grow immensely. We have to let the ego get exposed. When the ego gets exposed, we get to see it and seeing is everything.

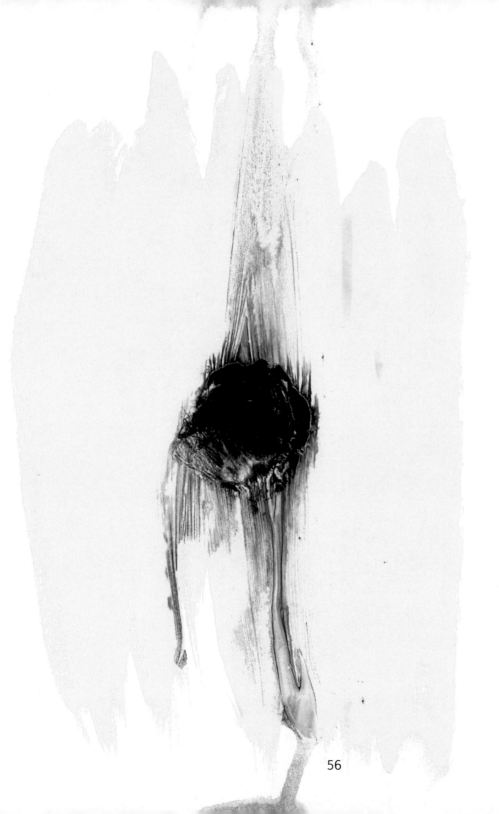

Fear
keeps us
tied to the
negative
past.

The whole
business
of the ego
is to be
better
than
others.

When we are miserable,
we make others miserable and
our subconscious loves it. Why?
Because in the subconscious,
we think we are better than others.
So if a situation is bad for me,
 it should be bad for others too.

If you think you are special,
you separate yourself from others.
When you are separate, you suffer.
Everybody is one with God.
How can you be a better
"one with God" than others?

The fifth chakra
is the bridge
between ego
and egolessness.

60

The fifth chakra is the peak of the ego, the peak of "I am better than everybody." So it is also the peak of separation. If you are better than everyone, you are separate from everyone also. The mind is also at its peak in the fifth chakra. But there is nothing wrong with this because when you become total in separation, you jump to unity. The same happens for the mind; from the peak of itself, it goes to no mind.

We just need one deep understanding to make this jump from the fifth chakra to the sixth—to move from separation to unity. That one understanding is that you *are* better than everyone else in your own way, which means you are the best of you.

Everyone is unique and the best of themselves, and at the same time, we are all one. So I could think, "I am the best," but that does not mean I am better than you. We are all the best, but not in comparison to each other. We are the best at being who we are. We meditate to slow the mind so we can have this deep understanding that takes us from separation and the peak of the mind to unity and no mind.

Ego resists because
it does not want
to be wrong about
all the things
it has been doing
for all these years.

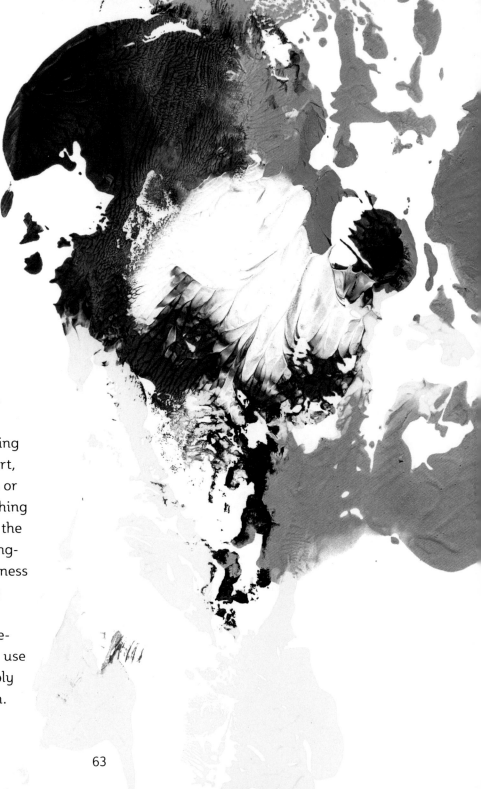

Why do people do something wrong? Because they lack understanding. And what is our response when we do something wrong? We can either fall apart, feel bad, and blame ourselves or others, or we can learn something about ourselves by looking at the situation more deeply, by bringing understanding and awareness to it. Don't waste your energy blaming yourself or others or defending the self. These all require a lot of energy. Instead, use this energy to look more deeply into yourself and the situation.

Existence does not know any failure. Failure belongs to the ego. But we cannot become aware of ourselves without what we view as failure, because it is only when we fail that we become interested in looking at ourselves and our egos. It is only through looking, witnessing, that we get to see the tricks and games of the ego and how destructive they are. We see how, ultimately, the ego caused our failures. The good news is that once we learn to see or witness our ego and its destructive ways, the hard part of our work is done—it is all downhill from there—and our path becomes easy.

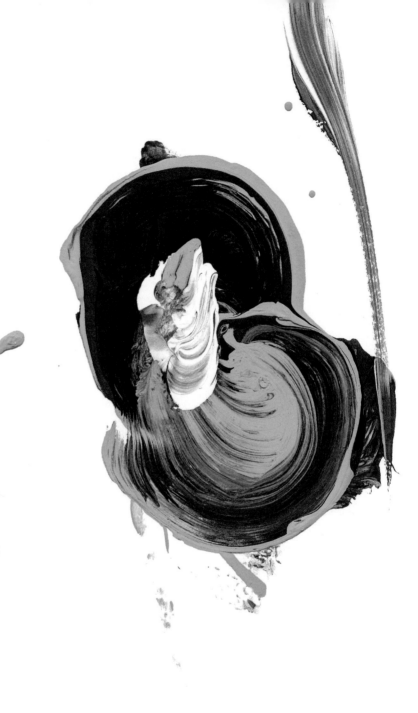

Existence is not overly
concerned with whether
you understand its lessons
right now. Existence is
patient. It gives you
unlimited homework
through life experiences
until you finally
understand.

The mind is like a stray dog: it wanders around all the time. The goal of meditation is not to stop the mind altogether, but to stop it when it needs to be stopped. We have to train the mind so it is under the command of our soul and not the other way around. We train it so that when we want to meditate, it becomes quiet. Other times, it can wander around as is its nature. And why do we want to stop the mind? When the mind becomes quiet, we can connect to our inner where we always know what to do. Confusion means that we do not have control over our mind. We get confused by all the different messages the mind bombards us with.

Confusion is
the beginning
of understanding.

The mind creates our reality, but our reality is different from the truth. Whatever is happening on the surface is the reality that our mind has created, but it is not the truth. It is only when we go deeper that we see the truth, the Beyond. It is only when we become aware that the mind creates reality according to the truth. Otherwise, it creates a reality based on our beliefs and conditionings. For example, the mind of a person who is aware creates love as his reality, because love is the essence of the Beyond or the truth. But the mind of a person who is not aware creates misery, because misery is the result of illusion (wounds, conditionings, beliefs). That is why there is so much emphasis on awareness, on a spiritual path, because when the mind is not aware, it creates suffering. Originally, the mind is given to us to create what we need according to the truth, but because we are unaware, our mind creates problems and sufferings instead.

If your life becomes too complicated, it is hard to see how your mind works. You focus on all the challenging situations and the mind continues to get away with its mischief. Simplify your life and you will see how the mind works. The mind wants to create challenges and problems over even the smallest things. For example, you are cooking dinner and all of the sudden your mind tells you,"Oh, it's getting late." Then, for the rest of the time you are cooking, you feel tense for no good reason. It is easier to see the habit of the mind when your life is simple. You just have to pay attention to it. Awareness is the key to getting out of the mind. As we watch the mind, the challenges it creates will lose their attraction for the ego. The only reason the ego is attracted to them now is because we cannot see that they are created unnecessarily by our minds, and we fall into them.

When things are simple, we don't need the mind so much. When they are complicated, the mind has to come in; we invite the mind in—things become mind intensive. Simplicity is intelligence. That is why children are more intelligent than adults. Their minds are clear and simple. A complicated mind becomes stupid, confused, unclear. It argues and creates tension. It believes that to look intelligent, it has to oppose others all the time. It is hard to be with.

People with simple minds are easy to be with. They are so beautiful, so uncomplicated, so refreshing and fun. Being with them is all space, and love happens. But when we bring in more mind, things are not simple anymore; space is taken away. What's left is heaviness and dullness.

70

We think because
we don't understand.
When we understand,
the mind stops.

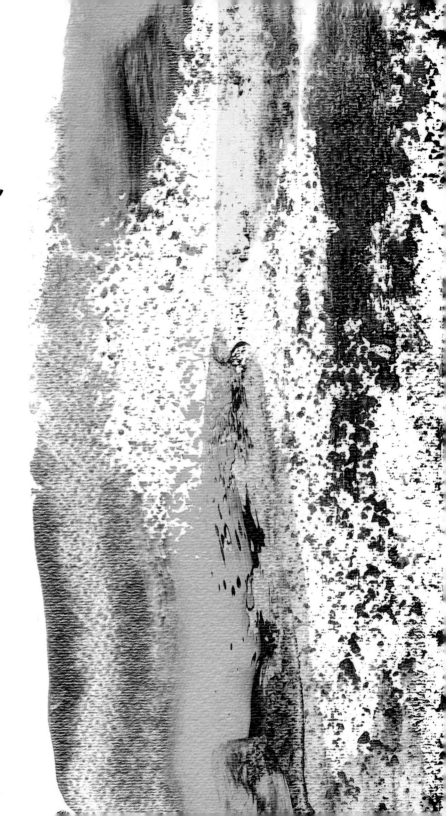

As soon as you
refer to your mind,
you lose the moment.
Then you can't be
creative and you
can't enjoy.

When you come to the moment,
you can see the games of your ego.
As soon as you see your ego,
you will be surrounded by prana
(energy). You become refreshed.

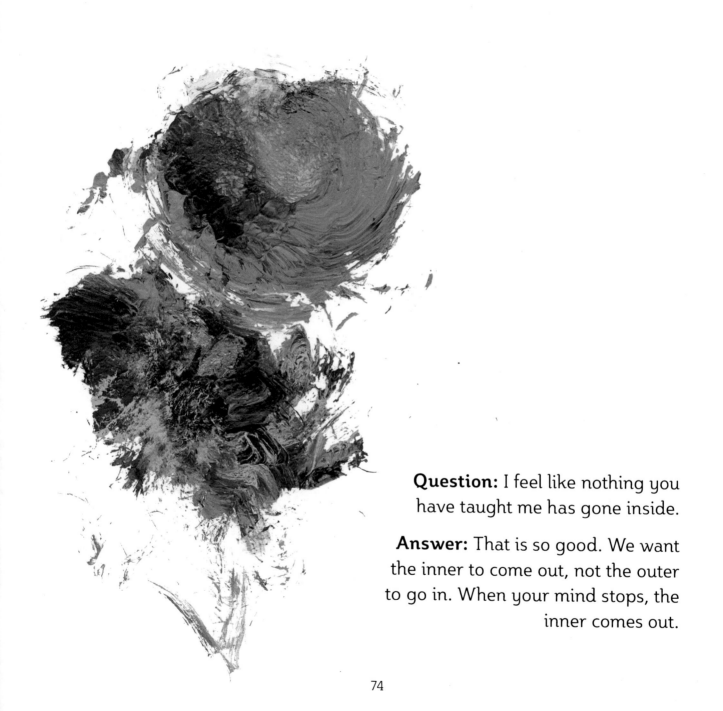

Question: I feel like nothing you have taught me has gone inside.

Answer: That is so good. We want the inner to come out, not the outer to go in. When your mind stops, the inner comes out.

Expressing is the first step in understanding. If you cannot witness and understand, the next best thing is to express yourself. When we express, we bring the matter up to the surface where we can see and understand it. We get a chance to look at a problem and talk about it, which leads to understanding. As we grow, we get to the point where we don't need to express to understand; we are aware enough to see and witness without expressing. Our witnessing leads to understanding, so there is nothing to express. When we witness, we go to understanding directly.

When you share in a group, you watch yourself because you are afraid of what other people might say. You pay a little extra attention to what you say. You are more aware. That little extra awareness is all it takes for you to change.

As we become
more and more aware,
we begin to cleanse
the blockages
in our being.

Blockages in any chakra are caused by energy that is opposite to the nature of that chakra getting stuck in that chakra. For example, the heart (fourth chakra) is the center of trust. It gets blocked by doubt. When we clean our hearts, the doubt gets cleansed, it gets pushed out of our heart chakra.

When one's energy is stuck in the heart chakra, it can be really hard to work with and clean, because the heart is female and female energy always throws responsibility onto others. When you think what you are feeling is somebody else's fault, it is very hard to change that bad feeling. Plus, because the heart is female, it is lazy by nature—it really doesn't want to change anything. If you can move the energy up to the fifth chakra, however, it is very easy to clean, because the fifth chakra is male. The male takes responsibility, which makes it easy for negative energy to come out. Our chakras alternate from male to female, with the first, third and fifth chakras being male, and the second, fourth, and sixth being female. The seventh is neither male nor female. If energy is stuck in a female chakra, the best way to work with it is to somehow bring it up to the next chakra, which is male, where the chance of becoming total is higher.

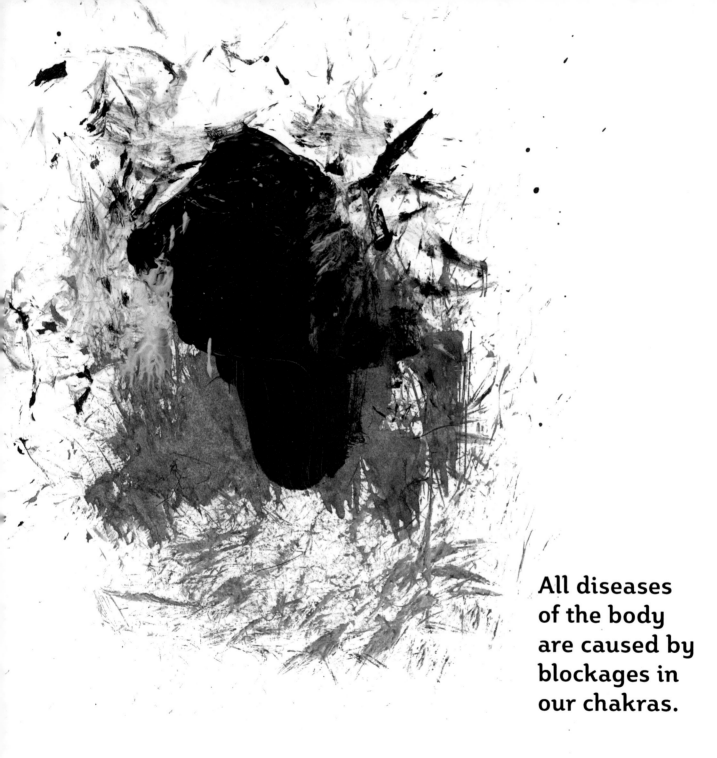

All diseases
of the body
are caused by
blockages in
our chakras.

When we go from a
lower chakra to a higher,
we enjoy, we feel high.
When we drop from a
higher chakra to a lower,
we become tense and
feel low. We are in hell.

81

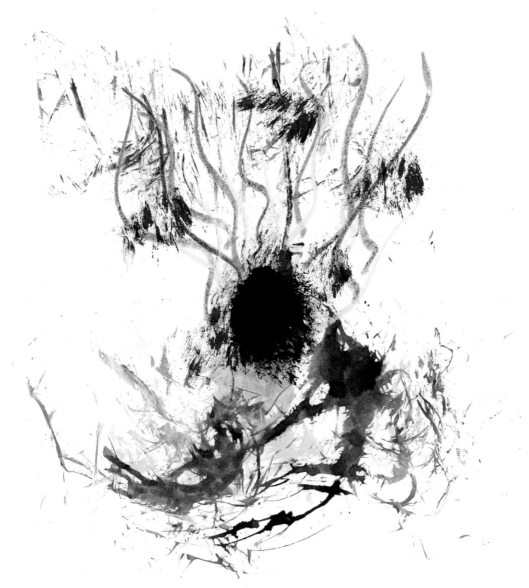

We are tense;
that is why we have problems.
It is not that we have problems,
so we are tense.

When you are
balanced and centered,
you lose karma.

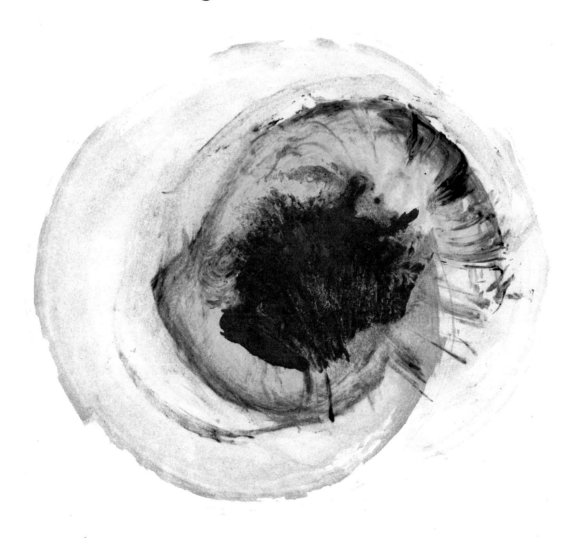

At first, when we come to the path, the male and female energies inside of us are polluted; they are sick, weak, and at odds with one another. As we work on ourselves, these energies become strong and clean. The final step is to adjust and balance these two energies. Imagine a broken-down car. To get the car running again, first you have to repair all the individual parts of the car that are broken. Then you have to adjust and tune the car, so that everything works in harmony with everything else.

So how do we balance our male and female energies? There comes a time on the path when you learn that you have to let go and let Existence take care of your growth. That does not mean that you just hang out and wait for growth to happen. You still have to participate in you growth. It is like the car. When it's broken, you take it to the mechanic and he fixes it for you, but you have to get it to him, and you need to know your car and have the awareness that something needs fixing. Finding the balance between these two (letting go and efforting) is the balance of the female and male. You don't push and you don't give up either.

So how does this work in us? The way we adjust and balance our male and female is by understanding subtleties. If you understand long enough, you gather enough understanding that all of a sudden you become totally balanced. Enlightenment happens. Just like water—you heat it and heat it and at one point it evaporates. This is the sole reason we have taken these understandings and put them in a book.

When we focus on doing something totally, we become more male. It seems unbalanced, but if we become completely total in something, without any restrictions, all of a sudden we go to the Beyond. We don't need to become female to balance this maleness. Total male goes to the Beyond which is the ultimate female. So we should not hesitate. Be total.

86

The struggle between
male and female
(logic and emotion) is what
makes a relationship strong.
That struggle brings strength
to the moment. It makes the
space around it strong.
If that tension is gone,
life becomes
boring and empty.

Controlling is necessary to
do anything. We just have to
mix the right amount of
control with the right amount
of let-go to be able to
do things with softness.

If you are imbalanced, you do not
want to hear criticisms of yourself.
If you are balanced, you say,
"Thank you," whether
they are right or wrong.
Balance brings acceptance.

When we argue, it is all
about "me" being right
and "you" being wrong.
It has nothing to do with
the truth anymore.

90

The moment
we defend ourselves,
we lose the truth.

91

It is pointless to argue, because you cannot convince anybody with argument. The best you can do is silence the other, which means they repress. This repression will only make them more angry. Then, at some point, they will have to get revenge. This is not a good situation. We think by arguing, others will understand us and our views, but when someone's heart is closed, which it will be in an argument, they are not open to hear us. If you want to hear and understand someone, you need to have an open heart and be agreeable.

We don't have problems
with others—only our
conditionings have
problems with them.

We often hear people say this person is too sensitive. However, the problem is not with sensitivity. As a matter of fact, sensitivity is very advanced and is very much needed for our personal growth. Sensitivity causes us to see things a little bigger than they are, and that is a great quality for our inner journey. The problem is with our conditionings that consider certain things good and others bad. Because the sensitive person sees things bigger than they are, these conditionings get triggered more easily, which then causes the sensitive person to get upset more easily. But getting upset is the best way to know that our conditionings are getting triggered. All that is needed is for us to become aware of and pay attention to these conditionings, these shoulds and should nots, so we can stay centered and free ourselves from them as they arise.

Sensitivity is tricky. On the one hand, it can bring you down, but on the other, it makes you aware, which is really high. If you are sensitive and you do not have wisdom, you suffer. If you are sensitive and you have wisdom, you do not suffer; you see things more deeply.

Ignorance means
with the ego;
wisdom means
without the ego.

People's moods change all the time. Sometimes we are more female, sometimes we are more male, and sometimes these two are in balance with one another. When we are more female, we feel weak. When we are more male, we are more gross. When the male and female come together in harmony—when they become one—we become one and feel one with everyone and everything around us. When this happens we experience the exciting feeling of love; our hearts start throbbing with so much energy. This oneness, this loving feeling is strength and when we feel strong, we do not reject anything; rejection comes from weakness.

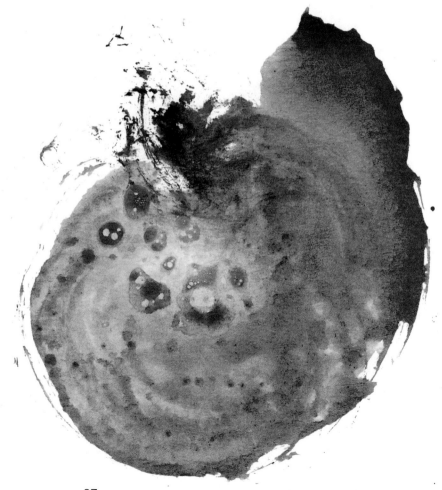

Crying has nothing to do with
sadness; it is all about aliveness.
Crying is our way out of sadness
into aliveness.

If we become vast inside, we see beyond hardships and nothing will bother us. In fact, there will be no more hardship for us. We get bothered by things because we still have limitation. The reason we have to go through so much hardship before we become enlightened is so that when we do become enlightened and feel the freedom of it, we really appreciate it. Inner freedom is so subtle that if we do not have anything to compare it with, we will miss it. We won't recognize and appreciate it. Enlightenment is the absence of heaviness. If we have not experienced heaviness, how will you recognize the lightness?

The keys to enlightenment
are meditation and love.
When we are meditating,
we are watchful.
When we have
reached love,
we accept.

100

Meditation helps us to be more aware,
which makes us more ready to
understand, and with understanding
the ego disappears.

As we understand the
subtleties of Existence,
the ego steps aside.

**Understanding
means the truth
is opening up.**

103

Any
understanding
leads
to
love.

Before an open heart becomes permanent, it is a phenomenon that happens in the moment. So your heart could be open in one moment and not the next. At one point, when the subconscious becomes clean and pure, your heart will be open all the time.

When someone is
on the path of love,
it doesn't mean that
they are loving;
it means that because
they lack love, they
need to be given
a lot of love
in order to grow.

Perfection does not mean
that one is perfect.
It means one has deep
and total acceptance
for everything there is.
When we accept, balance
follows automatically.

The enlightened person has direct access to divine energy. He can go to the Beyond any moment, whereas other people do not have access to that energy whenever they wish. But enlightenment does not mean that a person is in some higher altered state all the time. Enlightened people are just normal people with their own imperfections, but they are happy with their imperfections. Most people are imperfect and do not like it, so they suffer.

Take life easily and
naturally—just as it
comes, with an attitude
of acceptance. Don't
impose yourself on life.

SOMETHING TO LEAVE YOU WITH

If I can leave you with one simple exercise to help on your journey to awareness and joy, it is this. Recently I talked to a student about her mother. She said that her mom's attitude and the way she behaves really bothers her. She asked how she could stay centered around her mom and not keep falling into getting bothered. I told her, "When something starts bothering you or bugging you, anything at all, leave that thing and pay attention to your breath. Just pay attention to your breath—in and out. If you're total in that attention, whatever is happening won't bother you anymore. If you're judging, you will stop judging. If you're getting angry, you will let it go."

When you pay attention to your breath, all of a sudden you are inside yourself, you are not out there to be bothered by others. You move into the most important thing in your life, breath. Without it, we die. Every time you feel yourself getting bothered by another, whether you are feeling angry, jealous, sad or whatever, focus totally on your breath. Inhale and exhale deeply. You can have your eyes open or closed. As you breathe, all the emotions we so easily fall into fall away.

You might think that to start paying attention to your breath and not to the person you're with is rude, but isn't it more rude to just get more and more angry at the person? With breathing, you gain centeredness. You can go back to the person with centeredness instead of anger. This technique will not only get you through some tough moments, but with practice, it will also grow your overall awareness, and with awareness comes freedom and happiness.

GLOSSARY

AWARENESS: In normal life we usually are not aware of our Being. We only associate ourselves with our thoughts. Awareness means becoming aware of our Being by stopping the mind. We can stop the mind with meditation, focusing, or experiencing a moment of deep joy or understanding.

BODIES OF THE SOUL: We humans have seven different layers in our soul. We call them the bodies of the soul. The physical body is at the center of these layers, while all the other bodies move outwards from this center like the ripples created by throwing a stone in a lake.

FIRST BODY: Physical Body

SECOND BODY: Etheric Body – The etheric body extends about one inch beyond our physical body. All the chakras are part of this body.

THIRD BODY: Emotional Body – The emotional body extends about three feet out from the physical body. It is the body that stores our emotions.

FOURTH BODY: Mental Body – The mental body extends beyond the emotional body, but the extent to which it and the rest of the bodies do so depends upon our spiritual advancement. The mental body carries our thoughts and relates to the mind.

FIFTH BODY: Bliss Body – Where ecstasy resides. The bliss body contains the information of the past and is about hearing the voice of Existence.

SIXTH BODY: Spiritual Body – The spiritual body contains the information of the future. It is about seeing the Beyond.

SEVENTH BODY: Nirvanic Body – This body is about joining with the universe, becoming one with God.

CHAKRAS: The chakras are centers of the soul. They sit in the spine and head and direct different aspects of being.

FIRST CHAKRA: The first chakra is primarily concerned with survival issues, money, the instinctual. The way the first chakra operates is through attachment.

SECOND CHAKRA: The second chakra is more about pleasure, sex, and the emotions.

THIRD CHAKRA: This chakra relates to power, control, and the mental body, the mind.

FOURTH CHAKRA: The heart center is concerned with trust, letting go, love and acceptance.

FIFTH CHAKRA: This chakra is involved in expressing and hearing: specifically hearing the voice of Existence.

SIXTH CHAKRA: The sixth chakra is also called the third eye, which sees the hidden aspects of Existence, aspects the other five senses cannot sense.

SEVENTH CHAKRA: The seventh chakra relates to dropping attachments to the material world totally, living in the divine with absolute freedom.

CLEANSING: Getting rid of the energies that are not subtle *(karma)* and are blocking our chakras, causing us emotional pain, discomfort, and misery.

CONCENTRATION: Means focusing. Sometimes meditation and concentration get confused. Concentration is the first step to meditation. We use the mind to beat the mind by focusing totally. When we focus totally, we use the mind intensively, so much so that all of a sudden, it stops and meditation happens.

CONDITIONING: Teachings from our parents, teachers, and the society in general that create our belief systems and personality.

CONSCIOUSNESS: The mind is divided into two parts: the part we are aware of called consciousness and a much larger part of which we are not aware, the sub- or unconscious. The subconscious controls much of our feelings and reactions automatically without our really understanding why.

ECSTACY: A state of being where all the darkness of the soul is gone, leaving tremendous satisfaction or joy. Enlightenment is a state of everlasting ecstacy.

ENLIGHTENMENT: Simply put, the individual is in charge of, or has conquered, his ego and is in direct contact with Existence. His consciousness is lit up.

EXISTENCE: Existence includes everything in the universe from the material, animal, and the human to the emotional, mental, energetic—everything. We use this term almost synonymously with God, except that we are not separate from Existence. We are a necessary and vital part of the whole. It includes the deepest levels of understanding to the most shallow, and includes all aspects of human behavior, regardless of how we judge these behaviors as good or bad, valuable or not valuable. All is essential to the whole.

GOING TO THE HEART: Being in the heart or going to the heart means our kundalini energy rises from the first chakra up through the spine, passing all the lower chakras as it goes. As we travel higher up this main artery of the soul, the pathways become more subtle. So the energy can only continue to climb based on how subtle it has become. When we are stuck in the lower chakras, we feel that we are not safe enough. We believe that we need to control the things around us. To do this we use the mind. A lot of energy is used by the mind for thinking, which causes emotional pain, unhappiness, and a feeling of heaviness. Feeling love is the key to making the energy subtle enough to climb to the heart chakra and higher, which brings feelings of love, gentleness, and let-go. This is what we call going to the heart.

KARMA: Karma is a negative energy that creates blockages in the soul and the body.

KUNDALINI: The source of our personal energy, sitting in the first chakra. It is also called the energy of our life or the energy of the soul.

MALE/FEMALE: The kundalini energy is broken into two parts, male and female, regardless of whether you are a man or a woman. The left side of the body is governed by the female energy and the right side is governed by the male.

MEDITATION: This is a state of no mind, but when we talk about meditation, mostly it means creating situations to help the mind to stop, like sitting in silence and closing the eyes.

PRANA: The energy of Existence that we take in from our surroundings by breathing, eating, etc.

SUBCONSCIOUS (UNCONSCIOUS): Subconscious is below the conscious. Many paths divide the subconscious into subconscious and unconscious, but for general understanding, subconscious and unconscious are the same thing, unless you want to dissect them for different points of understanding. For example, subconscious is the new material that has been put in the basement of our mind. Unconscious is the older material, even from our last lifetime.

TOTALITY: This is becoming as intense, as completely focused as possible in whatever we are doing or feeling.

TRANSFORMATION: Transformation is when the mind stops, for whatever reason, and in result some blockages open up. Deep understanding will cause the mind to step aside. The ego also steps aside when the mind stops and our kundalini energy moves to the heart or higher, allowing for deep peace, joy, and ecstasy. Consequently, we experience inner opening and change.

Paintings by Sharam
View and purchase giclée prints

Visit:

SharamLove.com